HEINEMANN CHILDREN'S REFERENCE
a division of Heinemann Educational Books Ltd
Halley Court, Jordan Hill, Oxford OX2 8EJ

OXFORD LONDON EDINBURGH
MELBOURNE SYDNEY AUCKLAND
MADRID ATHENS BOLOGNA
SINGAPORE IBADAN NAIROBI HARARE
GABORONE KINGSTON PORTSMOUTH NH(USA)

ISBN 0 431 00735 7

British Library Cataloguing in Publication Data
Lambert, David
  Weather and climate
  1. Weather
  I. Title II. Series
  551.5

Designed by Julian Holland Publishing Ltd
Colour artwork by Tony Gibbons
Picture research by Karen Gunnell

Printed in Hong Kong

91 92 93 94 95 96 10 9 8 7 6 5 4 3 2 1

Photographic credits
t = top *b* = bottom *l* = left *r* = right

Cover: Science Photo Library
p2 ZEFA; 5*t* South American Pictures; 5*b* Barnaby's Picture
Library; 6*b* Thames Water; 7*t* Shell; 7*b* M.J. Hooks; 8*b* ZEFA; 9*t*
Crown Copyright; 9*b* The Aviation Picture Library; 10*b* Science
Photo Library/NASA; 11*t* Science Photo Library; 13*t* Science Photo
Library/Hank Morgan; 13*b* European Centre for Medium Range
Weather Forecasting; 14*tl* US Department of Energy; 14*tr* Science
Photo Library; 14*b* US Department of Energy; 16*t* Frank Lane; 16*b*
USAF Cambridge Research Lab; 17*b* ZEFA; 18*t* ZEFA; 19*t* Dr R.
Vamos; 19*b* Barnaby's Picture Library; 20*b* Allsport/Mike Powell;
21*t* and title page Michaelis Francis le Roith Architects; 21*b* Bryan
and Cherry Alexander; 22*b* Science Photo Library/D.R. Peel; 23*t*
Bridgeman Art Library; 23*b* Ardea; 24*t* ZEFA; 24*b* ZEFA; 25*t*
Frank Spooner; 27*t* C.J. Gilbert/British Antarctic Survey; 27*b*
ZEFA; 28*b* Mark Edwards Still Pictures; 29*t* Science Photo Library/
NASA; 29*b* Science Photo Library/Prof. S. Lowther; 30*b* ZEFA.

Note to the reader
In this book there are some words in the text which are printed in **bold** type. This shows that the word is listed in the glossary on page 31. The glossary gives a brief explanation of words which may be new to you.

WEATHER and CLIMATE

David Lambert

HEINEMANN

Contents

The weather factory

The world is rather like a factory where weather is made. The materials needed to 'make' weather are moisture, or **water vapour**, and air. These materials are the gases around the Earth, or its **atmosphere**. The Sun's energy warms the air and this creates winds that spread the heat and the water vapour around the world. When water vapour cools, it forms clouds, rain, snow, hail, dew and frost.

The restless atmosphere
The parts of the Earth that are closer to the Sun are heated more by it. The Earth is round, so the air over the Equator is hotter than that over the North and South Poles.

The hot air over the Equator thins, and grows lighter. This low-pressure air rises, spreads north and south, then cools, sinks and becomes denser. It forms belts of dense, high-pressure air in the subtropics. This air in turn becomes the trade winds that blow back to the Equator.

In the polar regions, in the far north and the far south, warm and cold air masses meet along an invisible zig-zag line, the **polar front**. Spinning masses of low-pressure air called **cyclones** or depressions form. These create air

▽ **The Sun's rays pass through more air to reach the Earth's poles than to reach the Equator. The rays are more thinly spread when they reach the poles. This means that the Equator is much hotter than the poles.**

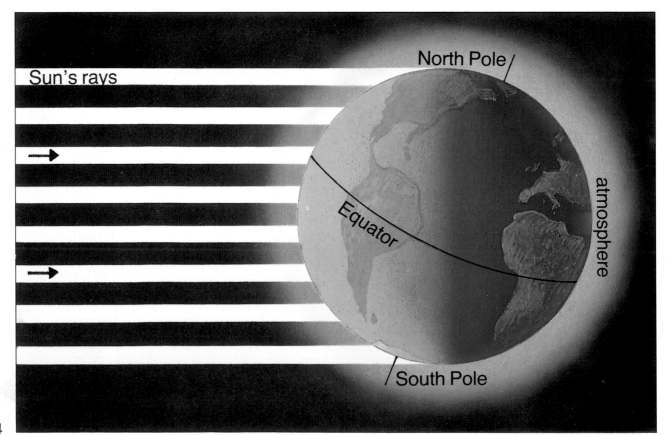

Sun's rays

North Pole

Equator

atmosphere

South Pole

4

△ **Holiday-makers from cool climates flock to sunbathe on warm, sunny beaches.**

movements, known as westerlies, that whirl eastwards. Sometimes a high-pressure air mass called an **anticyclone** blocks their path. Anticyclones counter the effect of a westerly and bring dry settled weather.

Understanding the weather

The usual weather of a place recorded over many years is known as its **climate**. Weather and climate affect our lives enormously. Changes to the usual weather pattern may either kill crops, or cover land in ice or water. It is important that we understand exactly how weather and climate work, if we want to avoid such disasters in the future.

▽ **This damage was caused by a hurricane. Weather forecasters can see hurricanes building up over the oceans and can warn people to leave the areas most likely to be affected by the strong winds.**

Tomorrow's weather

Weather forecasts tell us what weather to expect today, tomorrow, and even next week. This helps people plan work or holidays. Sometimes, forecasts can even save lives. In certain situations, being able to see clearly what is ahead, or have good **visibility**, is vital if a disaster is to be avoided.

On the ocean wave

Weather buoys floating on the surface of the sea carry instruments that measure the swell of the waves and the strength of the wind. The information transmitted by the buoys helps forecasters predict the weather and issue warnings if bad weather is approaching.

Shipping forecasts warn ships of storms, fog or icy conditions at sea. Forecasts are also essential for people who work on offshore oilrigs. These huge platforms stand in the open sea, and strong winds often whip up waves that make working on the rigs dangerous.

▽ **This 520 metre barrier across the River Thames in London was opened in 1984. It protects the city of London from flooding during very high tides.**

Shipping forecasts are broadcast by radio at exact times every day, so that a ship or oilrig can tune in to get an update on the latest information. If bad weather lies ahead, a ship can sometimes steer around it. This makes many journeys safer, and often quicker too. On the oilrigs, a storm warning will enable the engineers to plan work that is suitable for bad weather conditions.

In the air

Before planes take off, their pilots have briefing sessions at which they are given the latest weather information. If there are strong winds or snow on the way, the pilots may plan a different route, or even decide not to fly at all that day.

Fog, cloud and icy conditions can prevent planes from taking off or landing safely. In bad conditions, air traffic controllers establish by means of weather forecasts which airports are clear for aircraft to land at safely.

Planes travel at altitudes that have their own weather problems. For example, **clear air turbulence** can cause a bumpy ride. The pilots need to avoid headwinds that blow directly against the course of the plane. Instead, they want to take advantage of tailwinds blowing in the same direction as the plane. Accurate weather forecasts can help airlines to make savings on both fuel and time, as well as ensure the safety of the passengers.

△ **Engineers on offshore oil-rigs schedule work on the sides of the rig only after listening carefully to the weather forecast.**

▽ **Thunderstorms can wreck a small aircraft because of the turbulance and the danger of lightning striking the metal fuselage. Storm warnings help a pilot to fly around them.**

Measuring weather

To prepare a weather forecast, scientists called **meteorologists** measure the weather. They do this on the ground, at sea and in the air. The weather is measured several times a day and the meteorologists use various specialised instruments.

Land-based instruments

The weather is measured on the ground at weather stations. Air pressure is measured with a barometer. An anemometer shows the wind speed and direction. A thermometer measures air temperature. A hygrometer measures the amount of moisture or **humidity** in the air. Rain is also collected to show how many centimetres of rainfall has fallen.

▽ **The instruments at weather stations provide information that is interpreted daily by weather forecasters for thousands of people around the world.**

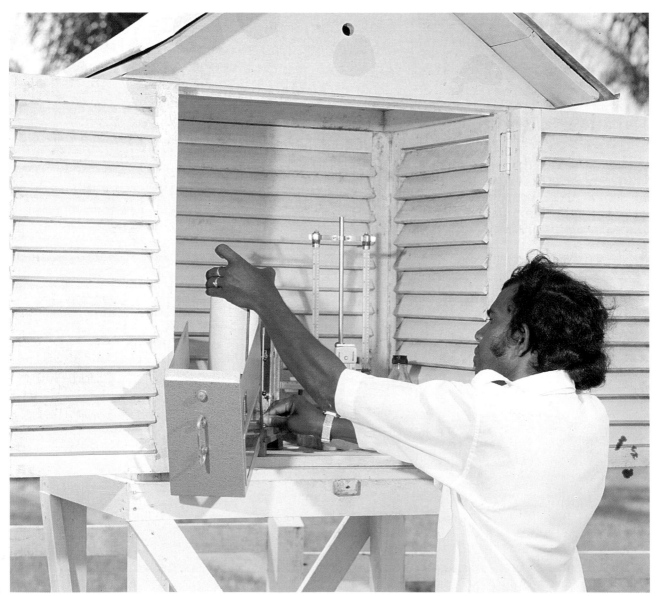

Some weather stations are equipped with **radar** equipment. This can be used to forecast bad weather by bouncing radio waves off rain showers falling many kilometres away.

All at sea
The temperatures of the surface of the oceans have a significant effect on the weather experienced all over the world. A change in the temperature can lead to abnormal weather patterns. Monitoring these changes can help with long-range forecasting. Sometimes it is possible to give warning of cyclones as much as two weeks in advance of them affecting a nearby land mass.

Measuring the upper air
The first signs of changing weather can be detected high above the ground. Weather balloons are floated up into the sky carrying a packet of instruments called a radiosonde. The radiosonde measures the temperature, pressure and humidity of the upper air. A radio broadcasts this information to the ground.

Extra information can be obtained by aircraft. Some planes on routine flights carry instruments on board that measure the weather. Sometimes instruments are added to the noses of aircraft which are then flown inside fierce storms to find out exactly what happens there.

△ **This balloon carries instruments to measure weather in the upper air. If the balloon bursts, the instruments are parachuted down and can be reused.**

▽ **Along the east coast of the United States and Canada, winter storms bringing heavy rain, snow and strong winds happen suddenly. This plane was used during an experiment to study how the storms develop.**

Eyes in the sky

Nowadays, weather satellites high in the atmosphere scan the changing weather far below. Each satellite is a collection of cameras and other measuring instruments.

Weather satellites are launched by or carried on rockets into space, far above the surface of the Earth. From there, they can observe a huge area of sea and land. The satellites pick up signals sent by weather buoys at sea. They send down information about the weather in the form of pictures and measurements of wind and temperature. This information helps to make weather forecasting more accurate.

Satellites

There are two main types of weather satellite.
Geostationary satellites stay above one spot on the surface of the Earth. They fly about 36 000 kilometres above the ground. Five of them, spaced out above the Equator, can keep watch on most of the Earth's surface.

Polar-orbiting satellites remain in one spot in space, and the world keeps turning below them. In effect, they travel around the world from north to south and back once every 100 minutes. They orbit at only 850 kilometres above the ground. This means that they have good close-up views of the Earth. Polar-orbiting satellites observe all the Earth's surface at least once every 12 hours. Two of them are able to keep track of all the world's weather.

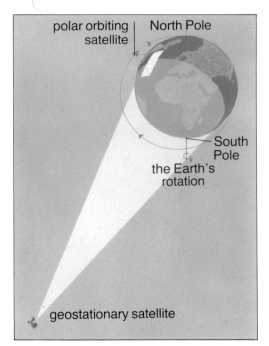

△ **The orbit of a polar-orbiting satellite takes it over both the Arctic and Antarctic regions. Geostationary satellites above the Equator, on the other hand, can scan an area from 50°N to 50°S.**

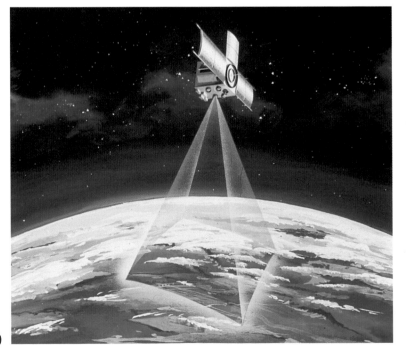

◁ **This weather satellite is full of instruments that are powered by solar energy. Satellites can even take photographs at night using infrared cameras.**

△ This picture of Japan was taken from space by a weather satellite. Colour-coding is used to show the different features, such as yellow for the clouds and red for Japanese territory. The Russian coastline is shown in green.

Messages from space

Weather satellites carry instruments called radiometers. Some radiometers measure the light from the Sun that is reflected back from the cloud, land or sea surfaces below them. Other radiometers measure the heat emitted. These last type are called infrared radiometers and are used to observe cloud patterns and the differences between the hot and cold layers in the atmosphere. Infrared radiometers are particularly useful at night or in bad weather conditions.

Both types of radiometer show how and where clouds form and move around. Other instruments on board the satellites measure air temperature and humidity at different heights above the surface of the Earth.

Satellites beam their information down to weather stations on the ground. Receiving equipment picks up the invisible signals and shows them as contrasting dark and light patches on television screens. Sometimes the images show the world as a person in space would see it, but in black and white. The pictures can be colour-coded, too, with hot and cold areas appearing in different colours.

11

Predicting weather

Thousands of weather measurements are used to give one forecast. The measurements are often taken from places right around the other side of the world. The World Meteorological Organization encourages countries to share their weather news, which is then brought together in central forecasting offices. There, supercomputers use the measurements to calculate how the weather will change in the near future.

A worldwide network

To predict weather, a forecaster imagines the surface of the Earth marked off in a grid. The corners of the squares of the grid are called gridpoints. These might be 100 kilometres apart.

The forecaster's first job is to measure the weather at each gridpoint. This means working out the air temperature, pressure, humidity, and wind speed and direction. Then this is worked out for up to 20 levels in the air above each gridpoint. The forecaster works out how all this could change in the next 10 minutes, then the next and so on. Forecasters call these time gaps **time-steps.**

▽ **Weather stations, balloons, aircraft, satellites, ships and radar collect weather information. This information goes to weather centres, where it is used to forecast the weather for the following day.**

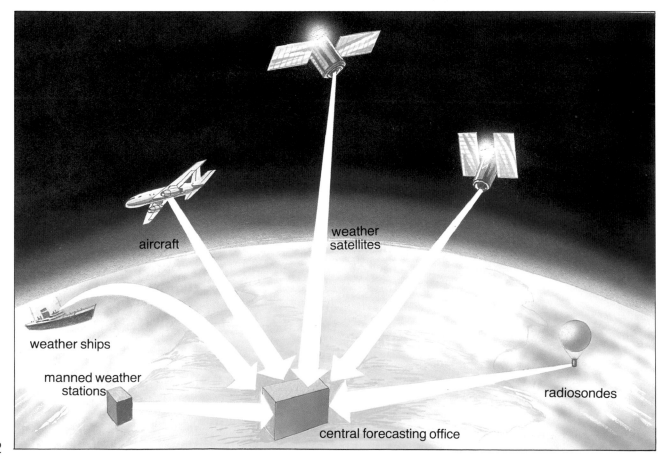

aircraft

weather satellites

weather ships

manned weather stations

radiosondes

central forecasting office

△ **Computers work out likely weather changes step by step. The great advantage of using computers is that they work at speed.**

Supercomputers

Forecasting the world's weather for one day means doing 500 million calculations. Only the world's most powerful computers can work that fast. Supercomputers work out their results as numbers. Changing sets of numbers can be translated into television pictures of clouds moving across sea and land. Or meteorologists can turn the computers' figures into weather charts. These have different lines and shapes to represent warm air, cold air, high pressure, low pressure, and wind speed and direction.

Supercomputers produce forecasts that are usually accurate for up to three days ahead. However, they can be unreliable for long-term forecasting because they magnify small mistakes.

▷ **This is the CRAY 1 supercomputer used at the European Centre for Medium Range Forecasting in Berkshire, England. Supercomputers can handle more than 50 million instructions in a second.**

Using weather

◁ **At this solar power plant in California, nearly 2000 mirrors beam reflected sunshine at a boiler on a tower. In the boiler (above), water turns to steam. This produces enough electricity to heat 1000 one-bar electric fires.**

▽ **The Mod-5B aerogenerator has a 100-metre rotor blade. In the 1980s this giant aerogenerator began supplying electricity to 1200 homes on the Hawaiian island of Oahu.**

Scientists can now do more than forecast weather. They can make weather work for us. They can use the energy in the wind and sunshine to heat and light our homes and factories.

Wind power

The world's winds produce millions of times more energy than the biggest power station. Modern 'windmills' can convert some of this wind energy into electricity. These **aerogenerators** usually stand on windy coasts or hills. One aerogenerator in Hawaii can produce enough electric current to work more than 3000 one-bar electric fires. Sometimes, wind turbines are grouped together to form **wind farms**. These are built where the climate is most suitable for the greatest production of energy. Engineers can store the wind turbines' spare energy in electric batteries until the power is needed.

Electricity from sunshine

Each week the world receives more energy from sunshine than all the energy hidden underground on the planet in the form of fossil fuels. Scientists have devised means to trap and use some of this energy.

In a **solar power plant,** many mirrors beam reflected sunshine at a water tank. The sunshine heats the water until it turns to steam. This spins the blades of a turbine which in turn generates electric current.

Electricity also comes from sunshine falling on thin wafers of substances like silicon. Groups of these wafers form **photovoltaic cells**. The energy collected by the cells can light lamps or be used to pump water.

The Russians want to use photovoltaic cells to fuel power stations in space. A space power station could send an immensely powerful beam of energy, or **laser** beam, to Earth. This would be a very effective weapon. There are also plans to build huge mirrors in space, which would beam down collected sunshine to be used as stored energy to provide power at night.

▽ **The Russians are developing a scheme to heat farms and cities in the USSR by day and night. They would set up enormous mirrors in space, two kilometres in diameter, and solar-powered satellites mounted with laser guns. These would beam the Sun's energy to where it is needed on Earth.**

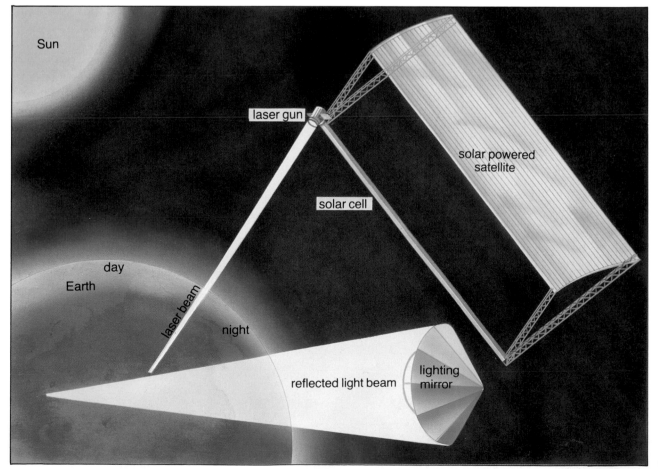

Sun

laser gun

solar powered satellite

solar cell

day

Earth

laser beam

night

reflected light beam

lighting mirror

Changing the weather

Bad weather can damage crops or injure people. Sometimes it is possible to manage the weather in such a way that the damage can be avoided.

Controlling the elements

On cold spring nights in California in the United States, farmers spray water droplets in the air above their orange groves. The droplets form a foggy layer that traps heat near the ground. This stops the frost from forming and damaging the trees.

There have been other less successful attempts to control the weather. Hailstones fall from thunderclouds and are often capable of flattening crops. Scientists have fired rockets into the thunderclouds in an attempt to break up the hailstones into smaller pieces of ice. This method has had a limited success. It is less expensive and perhaps more effective for farmers to listen to weather forecasts. If there is a warning of severe hailstorms, the farmers may change their minds about when to harvest a crop.

It would be very useful if it was possible to make rain, particularly in areas of drought. Scientists are experimenting at present with a new method. Planes drop

△ **Farmers would welcome a method of weather control which could avoid crop damage like this.**

▽ **Frozen carbon dioxide, or dry ice, produced water-ice crystals that fell from this cloud. As the ice melts, rain falls on the ground below.**

dry ice or silver iodide crystals on clouds. Moisture collects around the crystals and forms ice particles or water droplets. Some of the droplets join together, and they may fall as raindrops. This rain-making is called **cloud-seeding**.

Taming winds

In windy places, farmers grow high hedges or rows of tall trees around their fields. The trees and hedges slow down the fierce winds, or gales that can badly damage crops.

Violent winds called **hurricanes** or cyclones can wreck whole towns and cities. Attempts have been made to seed hurricane clouds in order to damp down the winds. However, it is very dangerous to fly aircraft through hurricanes, and there has not been much success with this method.

Tornadoes are the fiercest, most concentrated winds of all. A tornado is a spinning funnel of air. It travels over land and sucks up trees and buildings. Only a hydrogen bomb could tame a tornado, but this would cause more damage than the tornado itself!

▽ **Tall hedges and rows of trees act as windbreaks, protecting arable and pasture land.**

Weather changed by chance

It is possible to change the weather deliberately. However, the biggest changes come about by accident. Most of these make the weather worse.

△ **Fumes from thousands of cars helped to turn the air immediately above the city of Los Angeles in the United States a dirty yellow-brown.**

Murky weather

Fog forms when a layer of still, cold air lies close to the ground. The still air will trap the smoke and gas from factory chimneys. Sulphur dioxide gas and fog together make the dirty yellow mixture known as **smog.** Smog is a hazard because the harmful chemicals in it can damage people's lungs. It also eats into stone buildings. This damage can be avoided if coal and oil are not burned in factory chimneys.

Sunny cities with busy roads sometimes suffer from a yellow-brown smog that stings the eyes. The sunshine and the gas from car exhausts produce this **photochemical** haze. Filters on car exhausts can trap the gas and stop the haze from forming.

Deadly rain

Tall factory chimneys help to keep cities free from gases that poison, or **pollute**, air. Winds carry the gases far away. Unfortunately, this simply moves the problem from one place to another. Sulphur dioxide gas turns raindrops as acid as vinegar. The **acid rain** falls on fields, forests and lakes, some many kilometres away. There, the acid rainwater kills crops, trees and fish.

▷ Fish poisoned by the pollution in a lake in Yugoslavia.

△ Hot countries like Bangladesh often suffer floods during the monsoon season.

This need not happen. It is possible to fit factories and power stations with devices called **electrostatic precipitators.** These trap the substances that pollute air.

Too much and too little water
In hot countries, the effects of the weather are being felt in other ways. People have cut down forests in northern India. The trees no longer soak up the rain, so the rainwater rushes downhill. It washes away soil, and floods the valley of the Ganges River.

In parts of Africa, herdsmen and farmers make dry weather even drier. Herdsmen let too many animals eat the wild plants growing in dry soils at the edge of the Sahara Desert. Farmers try to grow more plants than the soil can feed. The crops die. Without the moisture escaping from plant leaves, the air gets drier. The rain becomes scarcer and the Sahara Desert spreads.

There is a way to avoid these imbalances. If more trees were planted, the Ganges would not flood, and the Sahara Desert would not spread.

19

Coping with climate

Naked, the human body is not built to survive the variety of temperatures experienced in most of the climates of the world. People have learned to protect themselves from heat and cold. They do this by **insulating** themselves against the weather.

Coping with heat

In hot climates, many people wear hats with large brims, and loosely woven cotton clothes. These shade the body, and soak up sweat, allowing air to flow around the body. White clothes are popular because they reflect hot sunshine.

In hot deserts, people used to build homes with thick walls and small windows. These keep out the Sun's heat. Modern homes in hot countries, however, can be light and airy with big windows. Electric fans and air conditioners keep the rooms comfortably cool, and the air pleasantly dry.

▽ **The Louisiana Superdrome is the world's largest stadium and an example of how efficient modern building can be. Inside, more than 90 000 people can stay comfortably warm and dry whatever the weather is like outside.**

Coping with cold

Living in cold climates, the problem is how to keep warm. People wear clothes that prevent the heat escaping from their bodies. Wool, fur and closely woven fabrics give the best insulation. Mountaineers and polar explorers wear several layers of wool or an artificial equivalent, and a woollen hat and woollen socks. Dark clothes help to absorb any heat from sunshine, so that people can get maximum benefit from what natural heat there is.

In cold countries, well-insulated homes are a necessity. In these areas, builders insulate modern homes in several ways. They lay glass-fibre blankets in the lofts. They may fill hollow walls with foam. The windows and doors of many houses have two sheets of glass with air in between. These **double-glazed** windows and doors are very effective at keeping the cold out and the heat in.

Nowadays, many houses in cold climates have central heating. However, there are some homes that have their air and water heated by the Sun. In these solar houses, sunshine warms water in panels on the roof. Large windows let in sunshine which warms brick walls and floors. These give out heat that warms the air indoors.

△ **In this solar home, water in the solar panels is heated by the Sun. The hot water in turn melts salts in a heat store the size of a refrigerator. As the salts cool and go solid again, they gradually release the heat which is used to supply all the warmth needed in the house for up to a week.**

▽ **These snowmobiles are used in places like Alaska or Canada to travel in conditions that defeat ordinary vehicles.**

Extremes of climate

Hundreds of millions of years ago, ice covered much of the continent of Africa. Stones got stuck in the bottom of the ice. As the ice moved, the stones left scratches in solid rock. The ice melted long ago, but you can still see the scratches that this **Ice Age** left behind.

The present Ice Age

Two million years ago a new Ice Age began. Great ice sheets covered Antarctica and much of North America and Europe. Over the following thousands of centuries, the world warmed and cooled several times. When it warmed, the ice sheets shrank. When it cooled, they expanded again.

Scientists can work out when the ice retreated and advanced. The clues lie in ice sheets and mud under the sea. The ice and mud built up in layers. In order to establish exactly what happened, scientists push hollow rods down through the layers. The rods are pulled up again filled with **cores** of mud and or ice. The mud and ice hold substances called **isotopes**. Different isotopes form at different temperatures. Examining the isotopes can show when in the past the world warmed up or cooled down.

▽ **Scientists collect ice cores from the Antarctic ice sheet. Ice buried deep down under the Earth's surface gives information about the weather experienced thousands of years ago.**

△ **In London in the 17th century, it was so cold that frost fairs were often held on the frozen surface of the River Thames.**

The Little Ice Age

Most northern ice sheets had melted by 10 000 years ago. However, they expanded again between about AD1350 and 1850. People call this the Little Ice Age.

This probably happened because the Sun gave out less warmth than usual. It is possible that this is connected with the lack of the dark patches on the Sun known as **sunspots**. There are no records of sightings of sunspots in the cold years between 1650 and 1715.

Volcanic eruptions, like that of Mount St Helens in the United States in 1980, have also altered climates. Volcanoes hurl dust high up in the air. The dust stops some sunshine reaching the Earth. This means that the Earth cools.

Sudden changes

Sudden changes cause sudden hiccups in climates. Every few years a warm current appears in the Eastern Pacific Ocean. Fishermen call this current El Niño ('The Child'), as it appears around Christmas when people celebrate the birth of Jesus. The winds change, too. All this affects weather far away. El Niño years bring drought instead of rain to India and parts of Africa.

△ **In summer, winds that blow from the Indian Ocean bring heavy rainfall to India, and the countries nearby. These monsoon winds reverse the winter, flowing back towards the Indian Ocean, bringing warm, dry weather with them.**

23

Climates made by people

Today, people burn more fuel, farm more land and produce more chemicals than ever before. All this puts smoke, dust and other polluting substances into the air. Bit by bit these substances are altering the world's climate.

Our clouding skies

Some substances, pushed up into the air, could make the climate cooler. Smoke pours into the sky from factory chimneys. More smoke comes from forests where trees are burnt to clear the land for farming. From dry fields, winds whirl dust high into the atmosphere.

Sunshine has to pass through all this smoke and dust before it reaches the Earth. Smoke and dust might, therefore, make it harder for the Sun to warm the world.

Living in a greenhouse

In fact the world is getting warmer. This is because of the other substances we put into the air. Carbon dioxide gas is produced by burning coal, gas, oil and wood. **Methane** gas is given off by animal waste and from paddy fields. Carbon dioxide and methane let the Sun's heat reach the ground, but then they trap heat below them. Scientists call this the **greenhouse effect**.

△ **Smoke and fumes from factory chimneys are probably making northern skies cloudier.**

▽ **This picture, taken from space, clearly shows the huge areas of tropical forest which are either being cleared or have been cleared by burning. This adds carbon dioxide to the air, and makes the atmosphere grow warmer.**

△ **Crops died when the rains failed in the grainbelt of the United States in 1988. The greenhouse effect could make this rich farmland an empty, dusty wasteland in the future.**

△ **Much of Florida would be under water if the sea rose between four and eight metres.**

Drowning coastlines

The greenhouse effect has already warmed the world a little since 1850. Now this process may be speeding up. Temperatures may rise by as much as three degrees Celsius in your lifetime. They may rise by double that in chilly polar regions.

All this would change the world greatly. As ice sheets melt, the sea will rise and flood low-lying land. In the United States, half of Florida, as well as much of the Netherlands and part of India would disappear.

Meanwhile, some areas would get more rain than now, some less. The British Isles might get wetter summers, but the vast grain lands in the United States could dry up and turn to desert.

It is vital that we burn less fossil fuel. We should also plant more forests, as trees take carbon dioxide from the air. Only in these ways will the world survive the dangers of the kinds of climatic change that we are already experiencing.

25

Holes in the sky

In the early 1980s, British scientists noticed that there was something missing from the air above Antarctica each spring. That something was an invisible gas, **ozone.** Ozone is oxygen that has been changed by sunlight. This happens mainly in the layer of the atmosphere 15 to 50 kilometres above the ground, the **stratosphere**. Up there, ozone forms a layer right around the world. Our lives depend on it.

Why ozone matters

If you squashed the ozone layer flat, it would be a mere three millimetres thick at sea level. Yet the ozone layer does a vital job. It protects us against most of the Sun's **ultraviolet radiation**. Strong ultraviolet light can cause skin cancers. Even stronger ultraviolet light could kill almost every living creature on Earth.

Ozone turns the energy from ultraviolet light into heat. This helps to warm the stratosphere. Without that warmth, there could be harsh changes in the weather.

Cause and effect

Scientists became even more concerned when they discovered another hole above the Arctic. They blame holes in the ozone layer mainly on chemicals called chlorofluorocarbons or CFCs. Manufacturers use CFCs in such things as refrigerators, air conditioners and spray cans, or aerosols.

CFCs produce chlorine atoms. A single chlorine atom can break down many ozone molecules one by one. This may happen much faster than new ozone molecules are formed.

▽ **The hole in the ozone layer over the Antarctic grew disturbingly during the early 1980s and is still a cause for concern today.**

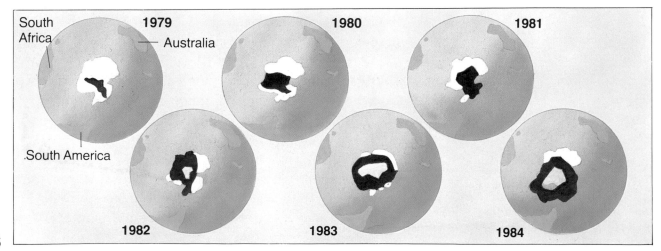

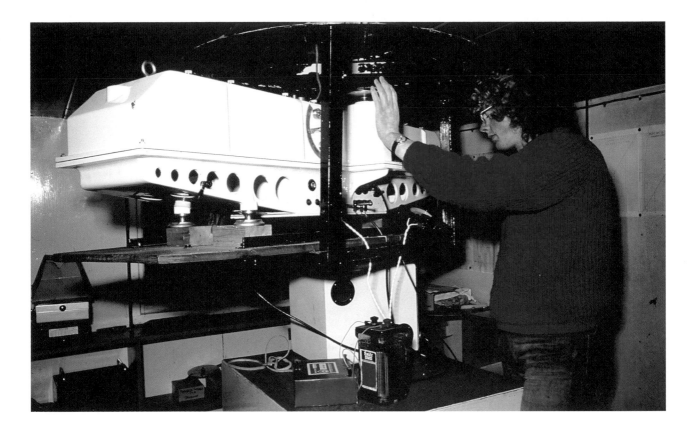

△ Scientists measured the ozone layer over the Antarctic from the ground and from the Nimbus 7 satellite high above. Every year teams of scientists visit the Arctic and Antarctic to carry out tests and to monitor the size of the hole.

Saving our protector

While ozone grows scarcer high above the polar regions, it becomes more plentiful down below. Animal waste, paddy fields and car exhausts all give off chemicals that form ozone. Some scientists think this might make up for the lost ozone. Others say the only way to protect the ozone layer is make fewer CFCs. In 1987, an international agreement was reached by many countries that will halve the production of CFCs, but it may be necessary to ban them altogether if we are to save the gas that protects us from the harmful effects of the Sun's rays.

▷ Some aerosols still have CFCs as the propellant in the can. However, more and more manufacturers are now using harmless chemicals instead.

Freeze or fry?

The gases that people pour into the air are already warming our world. Other changes will affect its weather in the future. Climates could become less mild than they are today.

Changing the atmosphere

People have the power to alter climates, sometimes in surprising ways. Chopping down tropical forests dries the air above them. This means that deserts may take the place of jungles. However, planting trees in deserts helps to make the dry air moist. When rain falls, fields and forests could replace barren sand and stones.

A nuclear war might damage weather all round the world. Hydrogen bombs would throw up enough dust to shut out sunshine for months or years. A **nuclear winter** like this would be cold and dark. Food plants would die and millions of people would starve.

▽ **These eucalyptus trees have been planted in Niger, Africa. Planting trees causes the desert air to be more humid, and makes it more probable that rain will fall.**

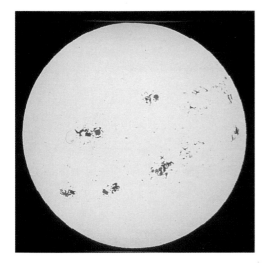

△ The marks visible on the Sun's surface, or sunspots, come and go, and the Sun's distance from the Earth alters. These changes could make the world warm up or cool down.

Changes in nature

Natural changes might alter climates most of all. Huge rocks from space could hit the Earth or volcanoes could explode. In either case, vast dust clouds could cool the world for months.

The cold of a new Ice Age might freeze the world. In the future, the Earth could be much further from the Sun, and this would make the world far colder than it is today. Some scientists expect the cold of a new ice age to come within a thousand years.

In the long term, there will be many changes. In millions of years time, the continents will have drifted far from where they lie today. The cold lands could have turned into warm tropics, while hot lands could become the polar regions of the future.

Five billion years from now, the Sun will swell to become a red giant and swallow the earth. Before that happens, rocks will melt and the seas will boil away.

▷ Mount St Helens poured huge amounts of dust and ash into the sky above western North America in 1980. The particles of dust reflected the Sun's rays, and so acted as a blanket, causing a noticeable cooling of the weather.

Concrete deserts

Cities have a climate of their own. Their climate is very similar to that of a hot desert. This is because there are few trees or patches of bare soil to soak up moisture, and then release it again to cool the air. Instead roofs, walls and streets soak up the heat from the Sun. In summer, you can fry an egg on some city pavements. Asphalt, brick, concrete and stone store heat. They slowly release it like a storage radiator. By day or night, in summer or winter, a city and the air above forms an island of heat.

City weather is unlike that of the countryside in many ways. Its air is hotter, dustier and drier. The city gets less sunshine and less snow than the countryside, but there are more fogs, more cloud and more rain in the city. As the warm air rises from a city it sets off thunderstorms. London's thunderstorms give that city nearly one–third more rain than falls on the fields and woods around it. Winds funnel down streets between the blocks of tall buildings, but the grouping of buildings helps to keep out gales, so cities tend to be less windy than the countryside.

▽ **This picture of New York has been taken by a satellite. It has been colour coded so the hotter city area appears blue against the surrounding land.**

Glossary

acid rain Rain made acid often by substances that escape from the chimneys of factories and power stations.

aerogenerators Machines with giant blades that are turned by the wind. The energy that the blades produce is converted into electric current.

anticyclones Masses of high-pressure air. They bring settled weather, often warm and sunny in summer, and cold and foggy in winter.

atmosphere The gases around a planet. The atmosphere of the Earth is the invisible mixture of gases called air.

clear air turbulence The air pockets and currents that planes meet at high altitudes.

climate The meteorological conditions, including temperature, rainfall and wind, that are usually to be found in a particular area.

cloud-seeding A method by which dry-ice crystals or silver iodide smoke are poured into clouds, usually to try to make rain fall.

cores The solid rods of mud obtained by pushing special metal rods down through ice or the ocean floor.

cyclones Whirling masses of low-pressure air that bring rain or snow.

double-glazing A method of using two layers of glass with air inbetween to keep heat in a house, and cold air and noise out.

electrostatic precipitators Devices that remove impurities from the air.

geostationary satellite A satellite that stays above one particular point on the Equator.

greenhouse effect The warming of the Earth produced by some gases. They trap heat in a similar way to a greenhouse.

humidity The amount of water vapour in the air.

hurricanes Tropical storms with fierce winds. They often cause tremendous damage.

Ice Age A period of time when the ice sheets of the polar regions extend, and it is colder than usual.

insulation Material used as clothing or in houses that keeps heat in and cold out.

isotope One form of a substance which can exist in a number of different forms.

laser A concentrated and powerful beam of light energy.

meteorologists Scientists who study weather. The study of weather is called meteorology.

methane A gas given off by decaying substances.

nuclear winter The cold, sunless weather that would follow a nuclear war.

ozone A gas that is found in the upper part of the atmosphere, known as the ozone layer.

photovoltaic cells Cells that can turn sunlight into electricity.

polar front An invisible, shifting line around the world. A polar front forms where warm subtropical air meets cold polar air.

polar-orbiting satellites Satellites that orbit the world above the North and South Poles.

pollute To poison with harmful substances.

radar A machine that bounces radio waves off distant objects. It shows the echoes as blips of light on a screen.

smog A thick yellow chemical fog found over some built-up areas.

solar power plant A place where energy is obtained from sunshine.

stratosphere The cold layer of the upper air.

sunspots Dark markings on the Sun's surface.

time-step A time gap between two sets of computer calculations that are used for making a weather forecast.

tornadoes Twisting columns of air that whirl at up to 480 kilometres an hour.

ultraviolet radiation An invisible light, too much of which can damage skin.

visibility The greatest distance under certain weather conditions that it is possible to see clearly.

water vapour Tiny, invisible particles of moisture in the air.

wind farm A group of aerogenerators.

Index